The Ultimate Year Six Guide To Leaving Primary School & Starting High School

Cara Jasmine Bradley

The Ultimate Year Six Guide To Leaving Primary School & Starting High School

Leaving Primary School:

Hi there, year sixes!
Hands up who's feeling super *excited* about high school?
Hands up who's feeling super *nervous* about high school?
And hands up who doesn't have a clue how they're feeling about high school, but it's somewhere in-between excited *and* nervous?

In the months of June and July, you may begin to think more about leaving your primary school and moving on to high school. You may have even thought about it earlier. This is because you're at the end of a era - an era you know well, and have been used to since you were four years old.

This is one of the most exhilarating - and at the same time nerve-wracking - periods of your life, and you should enjoy every single moment of the transition, because both primary school and high school are *ace*!

Some may feel excited about leaving, others not quite so. When *I* left primary school, I was *upset* to say goodbye to the life I had known for the past seven years, *thrilled* to start my high school journey, *anxious* about the big change, and *extremely confused*! One of my friends said he wouldn't miss primary school at all, and couldn't wait

to start high school, but I think he was just trying to act tough in front of the lads!
It's *totally normal* to feel a mixture of emotions.

You must remember that however you are feeling, you are *not* alone. There are thousands of year sixes up and down the country going through the same thing as you are. There is no right or wrong way to feel about the situation – everyone will be reacting in their own way.

Here is the *ultimate* savvy year six guide to leaving primary school and starting high school, cram-packed with top tips on how to make the changes easier for you.

Top Tips For Handling Your Last Months At Primary School:

1) Don't spend too much time fretting about high school. Make sure that you enjoy your last few months at primary school, so that you will always remember it to be a happy time, not one plagued by unnecessary worry.

2) Keep a diary. Write down all of your feelings. Not only will this help to clear your head, but it will also be funny to look back on in a few years! I have such a giggle reading my year six diary now - it's hard to believe that the scandal of the century came about when one of the girls *hugged* her boyfriend after school... And I wish my biggest upset was still down to the canteen failing to serve *Smiley Face Potatoes* one lunchtime!

3) Talk to someone you trust about how you're feeling. This could be your Mum, Dad, school teacher, Grandma, or even your best friend. Sharing your feelings can help to lift a massive weight off your shoulders. I confided in my Grandma that I was a little apprehensive about starting high school, and she gave me some great advice, along with my favourite ice-cream dessert to 'cheer me up' which *definitely* made me feel better!

4) Speak with someone in the year above who went through the same procedure last year. Ask them how *they* felt. You may be reassured to know that they felt exactly the same as you do, but are now having the time of their lives in their new environment!

5) Try to make the most of your school. Even if you *are* looking forward to high school, you must remember that your primary school plays a big part in your childhood. Set yourself targets and work towards achieving them (things like *'Read a reception child a story,'* and *'Get all my maths homework right'* always go down well). Not only will *you* find this rewarding, but your teachers will be pleased, too. This way, you are getting something positive out of your time left.

6) Do the things you've never tried before. If you've always wanted to join the school dance club, play football on the field, or even have a second helping of jelly in the canteen, now is the time!

7) Make a scrap book. Write down all of your favourite memories and get your friends to write messages to you. Take note of what you had for lunch on your last day, and which song was number one in the music charts. Do funny profiles of all of your teachers and their trademark expressions. You could even draw a cheeky caricature of them – just make sure they never see it!

8) Got any memorable incidents coming up? Take photos! If you're having a year six leavers' disco, or a big last football match, take pictures to remember them, and stick them in your scrap book.

9) Ask your teachers if they have any hilarious memories of you. Were you the child who forgot it was non-uniform day and turned up in your school jumper that time in year one? Or were you the Wiseman who forgot

his words in the nativity play?
Your teacher will be more than willing to share these
fond memories with you, and you will be chuckling with
embarrassment in no time!

Your Last Day at Primary School:

This is the day that the emotions usually kick in.
On *my* last day at primary school, I was upset, but also
quite eager. I knew that when the bell rang at quarter past
three, a new beginning would unfold.
It felt *really* weird putting on my uniform for the last
time that morning. I think it was the last day that I ever
wore Velcro shoes, too!

Your parents may want to take pictures of you on your
last day, and I'm sorry to say that you'll just have to grin
and bear it! I bet it doesn't seem five minutes ago that
you were having your photos taken on your first *ever* day
at school. The photos my Mum and Dad took of me on
my last day are *so* cringe-worthy! I'm stood in the garden
with my arms folded, and a sort-of half smile on my face;
obviously *far* too cool for a full-blown toothy grin. I had
the most *tragic* fringe, teamed up with those awful
primary school socks - you know the frilly ones with the
blue and white checks around the top? Just take
reassurance knowing that however embarrassing your
last day photos are, they won't be as bad as mine!

Most primary schools have a special assembly on the last
day of term.
This usually consists of the year sixes doing some sort of
play, or impressions of the teachers (great fun!) which
the parents' can watch. This is the one opportunity you
will get to take the Mickey of your headmaster's constant
coffee drinking, or the banshee way in which the dinner
ladies shriek *"SECONDS!"* when there is food left over

in the canteen. My year six teacher had a habit of sighing and proclaiming *"Oh, it's like drawing teeth!"* when she was annoyed, and I did an impersonation of this during our last day assembly, which had her in stitches.
You will find you are so busy laughing at your classmates antics that you will temporarily forget any gloom you might have lingering.
Some schools may also give awards out to the year sixes, or a good luck present.

The afternoon will probably be dedicated to chatting and chilling out.
A lot of schools let other pupils sign the year sixes' jumpers and shirts, so you may well have an afternoon of reception children jabbing pens into your back!
(I actually still have my signed year six shirt! I can't believe that I once fit into something so *small*!)

As the bell marking the end of your time at primary school sounds at quarter past three, you may be feeling:

* Upset :,-(

* Excited :-0

* Nervous :-s

* Confused :-?

* Apprehensive :-$

From experience, this is usually when all the girls start

crying, and all the boys start cheering, (or trumping!) in celebration. On *my* last day, all of us girls hung around hugging one another and weeping, while the boys charged out to play football at the park, swinging their jumpers around their heads.

If you happen to be one of the more confident members of your class, be sensitive to how others might be feeling. It's great that you're so positive, but there will be people who are feeling worried. Spare a reassuring word, thank your teacher, and head off to enjoy your summer holidays!

For those who *are* feeling a little distressed; feel free to stay behind after school and talk to your teacher, who will offer you advice and comfort. Remember, they have watched many children before you make the transition, so are in a really good position to provide guidance.

When You Get Home From Your Last Day At Primary School:

Everyone will be feeling different on the evening of your last day. Some people will be so excited for the upcoming summer holidays that they will forget all about the fact that they've just had their last day at primary school. They'll probably head straight to the park for a celebratory game of football, or a trip to the ice cream van to *really* get the summer underway. These sorts of people are great to be around if you're feeling a bit down, as they will lift your mood and distract you from the emotional day.

If you're feeling sad, you may want to be on your own for a little while. You might like to sit and reflect on your primary school memories. You could do this by looking back through old photos, your scrap book, or listening to songs that remind you of primary school. *Don't* feel embarrassed if you cry - year sixes everywhere will also be feeling upset.
When you're ready, put on a smile, have a chat with your family, and treat yourself to an extra slice of cake at teatime.

Some people will be feeling thrilled to be starting high school. If this is you, then try and offer advice to your friends who may not be looking forward to it as much as you are. Another great way to cheer your friends up is by making lots of fun plans for the summer holidays. Hopefully they will be that excited about that trip to the cinemas that their mind will drift from primary school.

How about organising a little get-together with your friends? You could host a girly sleepover and discuss your favourite primary school memories. Add pizza, popcorn and plenty of gossip to the equation, and you've got a perfect night planned! This will help to take your mind off any sadness you may feel, and just being surrounded by your friends will really lift your spirits. You could even watch your old primary school Christmas plays if you have them on video – that will make a fair few people cringe!

(You think *your* Christmas plays are embarrassing? I was the smallest girl in my class all the way through primary school, and was actually cast as a *mouse* in the Christmas play one year! As if it wasn't cringey enough having to wear fake whiskers and a *tail* all night, I then had to squeak and scuttle across the stage in front of the *whole entire* school *and* all of the parents!)

If you're a lad, then how about planning a gathering at the local park? Ask everyone to bring food, drinks and footballs, and then prepare for an evening of sport and sweets! You will find that you're trying so hard to score that hat-trick that you won't have time to worry about high school.

The Summer Holidays:

I hate to tell you this, but the summer holidays between year six and year seven go *mega* quick! They will fly by in a blur of pencil case buying, frantic last minute uniform trying, and *lots* more photos (for your parents of their 'BIG' son/daughter).

Although it is understandable that you may spend a lot of the summer holidays worrying about your upcoming first day at high school, please try not to let the fear ruin your time off. Focus on all of the cool things you have planned over the holidays, and make it your best summer *ever*! Surround yourself with your family and your besties, and make magical memories to last a lifetime. Maybe a shopping trip with your BFF is on the cards? You could head into the town and pick out the *coolest* pencil case and pens so that you will be the absolute *envy* of your class at your new school! School bag shopping can also be a fun thing to do with your mates – will you go for the rucksack with your fave footy team on, or a trendy sports bag with a special pocket for your football boots?

On The Last Day Of The Summer Holidays, You Should:

* Pack your bag for your first day at high school. You should have a full pencil case, a notepad, a snack for break time, water, lunch, your purse/wallet, and maybe a mobile phone and house keys.

* Set out your new uniform.

* Arrange to walk to school or to the bus stop with a friend. That way, there's less chance of you getting lost, and you will feel more confident. Plan to set off at a reasonable time - you certainly don't want to be late on your first day.

* Eat a full, healthy meal. No matter how nervous or excited you're feeling, don't skip meals, as this could make you feel really poorly.

* Set your alarm clock ten minutes earlier than you intend to get up so that you have some spare time to double check you have everything you need before you leave. Whatever you do - DON'T oversleep!

* Have an early night. I know it sounds stupid and babyish, but no later than nine O'clock is probably best. Don't play on computer games or do strenuous exercise before sleeping - do something relaxing, like reading.

* If you *are* feeling anxious, make sure you talk to someone. Even if you find that the worries kick in after you've gone to bed, don't be afraid to get up and talk to your parents or siblings. They may well be feeling as nervous as you are.

Your First Day At High School:

When you wake up, even the most confident person will be feeling the same as you = **NERVOUS!!** :-S

Either your alarm clock or Mum will have woken you up (or your little sister, or next door's noisy dog...).

It's best that you have some breakfast, even if you don't usually. Have a glass of fruit juice, milk or water, with toast or cereal.

Have a wash (or a shower if you've got plenty of time), get your hair looking cute, and put on your new uniform.

Your parents may want yet more pictures of their 'Special, grown-up baby,' so you'll just have to smile and get on with it again.
It's a big day for your parents as well as you.

Double check you've got everything you need.

Set off a few minutes earlier than you planned just in case you get lost, diverted or forget something.

Once at your new school, try to find someone you know, even if it *is* that weird boy who used to pick his nose back in year three. At least you'll be with a familiar face.

Most schools will ask their year sevens to go to the hall on their first day, where you will be put into different forms.

When you've been allocated your form, your form tutor will most likely take you all back to her classroom. You will probably spend the rest of the day getting to know your new class, playing games, and swapping cool stories about your exciting summer holidays. *Lucky you!*

Primary School v High School: Which Is Better?

People have different opinions on whether primary school or high school is better, and for weeks - sometimes even months - you may miss primary school a lot. Others, however, settle into high school during their first week.
High school is a lot different to primary school, and they both have their advantages and disadvantages.

Reasons Why Some People Prefer High School:

* Curriculum wise, there is much more to offer at high school. When I was at primary school, we only did cookery lessons once a year, and made quite unexciting things like basic cornflake cakes. At high school, food technology was a weekly lesson for me. I got to make a variety of different dishes, such as burgers, American muffins, fruit salad, and yummy chocolate flapjacks!

* Textiles and Sewing: not many primary schools do these activities often, but you will find that they are on the curriculum at a lot of high schools. You'll hopefully get the opportunity to make things like cushion covers, bags and puppets. Channel your inner *Vogue* designer!

* There are more physical education options. Trampolining, swimming, badminton, lacrosse and hockey are just a few different sports to try!

* The quality of drama, dance and music lessons at a lot of high schools is phenomenal! Budding singers, dancers

and actors will be thrilled at the chance to perform in school productions. Certain schools even do talent competitions and *X-Factor* mocks, so performers will be right at home.

* Design and Technology gets a lot more complicated at high school.
You may be asked to design *and* build things like money boxes, clocks and sun dials, which you can take home with you and impress your family with!

* There are *hundreds* of new friends to meet! There will be at least 200 people in your high school year! If you've always loved dancing or cricket, but no-one at your primary did, then you're more than likely to find a new group of friends who share the same interests.

* You may even meet new cute lads/girls!

Going Back To Primary School:

You may still miss your primary school as the months at high school go on, but hopefully not as much.

If you choose to attend your old primary's school fairs, you may be shocked to see how babyish it feels to you now. You'll have grown up a lot, and now realise that if you *were* to go back to primary school, you'd feel very out of place.

There are lots of ways to still be involved with your primary school.
These include:

* Attending fairs.

* Helping out at the fairs. You could work on the lucky dip, bake cakes to sell, or donate some of your old toys to the second hand stall.

* Dropping off and picking up your little sister or brother.

* Email your old head teacher and ask if you can teach a certain year of children a hobby you enjoy (think football, or dancing). Not only will this put a smile on your face, but the children's too.

* Once you reach years ten or eleven (scary thought!) you may be asked to do *Work Experience*. You could go to your old primary school, and experience just what

your teachers had to put up with!

* Offer advice to other year sixes who are going through what you went through.

* Keep in touch with your old teachers; it may sound a bit geeky, but it will please them, and you will find that they will talk to you like you're an adult. You will seem so grown-up to them now.

Frequently Asked Questions:

Q. *I'm worried I'll get bullied. Is it common at high school?*
A. Bullying isn't a big issue at high school. Most people grow up a lot when they reach high school, so will find bullying *seriously* immature and pathetic. However, on the rare chance that you *do* get bullied, you MUST tell an adult you trust, who will sort it out. People who bully are *so* uncool and need to be taught the right way to treat others. Don't suffer in silence.

Q. *I heard a lot of people smoke at high school. Will I get made to smoke?*
A. No-one will force you to smoke. Smoking can be a problem at some high schools, but not usually in year seven. By the time you're in year eight, you'll know the trouble-makers in your year and know to stay away from them. If anyone puts pressure on you to do anything you don't want, tell a trusted adult (a parent, the school nurse, or a teacher). Smoking, like bullying, is not cool *at all*, and is really bad for your health, plus it smells *totally* yucky!

Q. *My older friend said the school nurse is just like an old fashioned matron! Will she be nasty if I'm ill and make me stay at school?*
A. Most school nurses are nothing like old matrons, don't worry! If you're very poorly, it is likely you will be sent home, but if the nurse refuses to let you go home, you must trust her. She will have had many years experience, and knows what is serious and what's just a

normal tummy ache. You can also talk to the school nurse about anything that may be bothering you (bullying, worries, illnesses). She won't tell anyone. You'll find the nurses' are usually kindly ladies, and many people make friends with their school nurses.

Q. *My biggest fear about high school is that I won't make friends!*
A. It is highly unlikely that you won't find *someone* you get on with amongst the 200 or more people in your year. Try joining clubs of interest and meet like-minded friends. Be confident and speak to people you've never spoken to before. If you see someone standing on their own outside your maths classroom, smile and approach them. Ask if they have the same maths teacher as you, and how they're finding the class. The conversation will flow from there and you will have *already* made a new friend! It is as easy as that! Just be yourself, be friendly and smile, and your genuine personality will shine through, and people will be drawn to you.

Q. *I am going to miss Primary School so much! How am I going to get over this?*
A. Believe me, you will not be the only person to feel this way. It took me a long time to get over leaving primary school. This is totally normal. Remember: this is a *huge* change for you. There is no rush to grow up or forget primary school, so take your time and don't be scared to tell someone how you are feeling. Change can be mega scary, but it isn't always a bad thing - you have to move on to make room for new exciting chapters in your life!

Q. *Some of my friends are going to a different high school. I'm going to miss them a lot. How am I going to cope without them?*
A. This is actually quite an exciting scenario! Just think - they will make a whole group of new friends at their alternative high school, and they'll inevitably introduce them to you when you all meet up. This means more new friends for you, on top of the ones you will have made at your own high school!

There are plenty of ways to ensure that you stay in touch with old mates. Make sure you make a note of everyone's addresses and phone numbers on your last day at primary school. Some people may have an email address or access to a parents email address that you can mail each other from to swap news. If a friend of yours has always expressed an interest in horse riding or swimming or football, why not suggest that the two of you meet up at the local stables or swimming baths or five-a-side pitch every week once you've started high school? That way, you can embark on a groovy new hobby together, *and* catch up with all the juicy gossip from your separate schools!

Q. *Is the work harder at high school?*
A. The work is a little harder, but you will hardly notice the change. Don't forget that once you start high school, you are a whole year older than you were when you started your last year at primary school. We learn more as we get older and we become capable of much more, even though we might not realise this at the time. If you find yourself struggling with any of the work set by your teachers, just tell them. Let them know what you are

finding challenging, and they will go through it with you in more detail until you are happy. You certainly won't be alone in this - everyone has their own strengths and weaknesses.

I was totally *pants* at science, and my teacher offered to give me a few extra sessions during lunchtime until I felt more confident, which was a massive help to me. At first, I was reluctant to give up half of my lunch hour to sit with a boring old teacher, but actually, in the end, it was worth it for the fact that I caught up and no longer felt stressed out in class.

Q. *Will I get loads more homework than I did at primary school?*
A. You won't get a great deal more, no. The homework set on your first week at high school is usually just to cover your workbooks in wrapping paper to protect them! If you ever find yourself overwhelmed by the amount of homework you have been given, let your teacher know and they may be able to offer an alternative, such as the option of completing some of it in school. Also let your parents know so that they can lend a hand.

Q. *High school looks so big! What if I get lost?*
A. Now I can relate to this, as I got lost on my first week at high school! In the hustle and bustle of the corridor, I got separated from my new friends and ended up walking up and down for about half an hour, long after the corridors had emptied of pupils. I was too shy to knock on a classroom door and ask the teacher where my Religious Education class was, so I continued walking

around, feeling very foolish and *very* scared. Luckily, a passing teacher found me and took me to my classroom. I was *really* late, but luckily my teacher was understanding, and the other pupils thought I was seriously cool for being so late! If this happens to you, keep calm and try and find the nearest teacher or older pupil to guide you in the right direction. If, like me, you *are* a little late to your class, explain the circumstances to the teacher. Chances are they will be used to this happening on the first week.

Q. *I'm really worried that I will forget my homework or my workbooks. What can I do to prevent this happening? And what will happen to me if I do forget one day?*
A. I found packing my bag the night before was a really useful way to ensure I had everything I needed. As soon as I got in from school, I'd empty my bag, then look at my timetable for the following day and pack all the things I was going to need. If you have homework due in the next day, get to work on it straight away so that you can get it out of the way and enjoy some chill time. Once it is done, put it in your bag so that it is ready to be handed in. Before you leave the house, double check you have definitely got everything. In the rare event that you do forget your homework or your books, don't panic. If it is a one-off, your teacher will probably just give you a warning as they will know that it is not something you do often. Just make sure that you don't forget it again, or you might end up with a detention. This is the worst case scenario; a detention just means that you will probably have to stay in the classroom at break or lunch and complete the homework again. If you *are* given a

detention at lunchtime, you should be given time to eat your lunch first, so don't worry about that.

Q. *Is the old fashioned rumor that older pupils flush year seven's heads down the toilets true?*
A. No, absolutely not! This has always been a silly rumor passed down to primary school students but I have never, ever heard of it happening.

A Short Story: *'Leaving Deergate'*
Cara Jasmine Bradley

Chapter One -
About Me, Polly Hendrix

My primary school is the *best* primary school in the *whole entire world*. I started at Deergate Primary School when I was four years old, and I left when I was 11 - that's *seven* years spent there! Looking back, my years there seemed to go so fast, but when I think back to all those times I counted down the days until the summer holidays or Christmas, time seemed to stand still.

I live in a really small village in the countryside, so therefore my whole school only contained 150 pupils. There were 31 people in my class, and over the seven years, we formed a tight clique. Of course, being in the countryside also meant that our school's surroundings were *totally* picturesque - I mean, who else can say that their playing field backs onto a meadow filled with ponies? Once, a local farmer left one of his field gates open and a flock of sheep escaped and ran onto our school grounds! It was *so* funny - we were in the middle of assembly and about *thirty* humongous, fluffy sheep came barging into the hall!

So much changed in those seven years.
My ambitions altered from wanting to be a pop star - the only female member of *One Direction* - to the desire to become a lady footballer.
My wish for a little brother or sister of my own so that I was no longer an only child was never granted, although

when I was nine, I received the next best thing when my cousin Amber was born. My Dad's brother, Ryan, and his wife Elena (my Aunty and Uncle) are really close to my Mum and Dad, and made them godparents of Amber.

Another *not so nice* change was that of my parents getting divorced.

It was so sudden. I mean, yeah, they argued a lot, but don't *all* parents?

I was only ten at the time, and I had gone to my Grandma's after school. When Grandma dropped me off at half past six that evening, the house seemed quiet and so... *empty*. There was no enticing smell of chicken dippers as was the norm, and the sound of Mum singing along to my Justin Bieber album was absent.

I called out to Dad, and I called out to Mum. Neither responded, although Trusty, my Alsatian, ambled along the hallway, claws scratching on the laminate flooring.

"Dad?" I yelled again, standing at the bottom of the stairs.

Uncle Ryan appeared at the kitchen door. He looked drained, and his eyes were big and red like Rudolph's nose. I'd never seen my Uncle Ryan cry before. My heart started to thud under my jumper.

"What's happened? Is it Dad? Mum? Are they in hospital?" I demanded anxiously, dreading the answer.

Grandma stood behind me, biting her lip, her furrowed brow giving away her seventy-two years.

"Erm... Do you mind sitting down a minute, Polly?"

I backed into the sofa, dropping down like a stone, my legs turning to jelly.

Uncle Ryan knelt down in front of me. He couldn't quite

meet my eye, and that worried me. He was so like Dad: super tall, chubby, and *always* with a goofy smile on his face. There was no goofy smile that day.

"There's been an argument. A bad one. Your Mum and Dad have decided to... Well, they've..." Sighing exasperatedly, Grandma marched over to the sofa and sat down next to me.

"Polly... Mum and Dad have had a bit of a fall out. Sometimes, that's what happens to grown-ups who have been together for a very long time. They've decided it's best for them - best for *you* - to have a break."

"Are they going to Portugal?" I gasped, remembering how much fun we'd had last year on our summer break in Portugal.

My Uncle looked pained and rubbed the space in-between his eyes as if he had a terrible headache.

"To Portugal?" Grandma repeated. "No! Whatever gave you that idea? Your Mum has rented a flat on the other side of the town."

"And Dad, where's *he* going to live? Where am *I* going to live, Grandma?"

"Polly, what are you talking about, love? Your Dad is going to live here, with *you*. Your parents don't want a break from *you*. They both still love *you* very much. It's just, they need a little space from each other." I blinked.

"Will I still get to see Mum on my birthday? And at Christmas?"

"Of course you will!" Grandma sounded a bit choked, like she might be trying hard not to cry. "You'll get to see her *whenever* you like! We're going to do whatever we can to make things as normal as possible for you."

I looked at Uncle Ryan.

"Can I still visit you and Aunty Elena, and Amber?"

"You're welcome at our house *anytime*, Polly. The only thing that is going to change is the fact that your Mum is going to be living somewhere else for a while, just so her and Dad can have some space."

"Where's Dad now? He's left too, hasn't he?" My voice rose in panic.

Uncle Ryan pulled me into a hug.

"Stop being so silly, Polly!" Grandma snapped, as if it was *my* fault that I didn't understand what was going on.

"You're *not* silly, Polly, you're a good kid. Your Dad *hasn't* left, don't you worry. He's just helping Mum settle in."

As strange as my new life initially felt, I slowly got into a routine.

Every Friday after school, Aunty Elena would pick me up, along with Amber in her pushchair, and I'd get an overnight bag together and go to Mum's.

Mum didn't *want* to see Dad, she *didn't* want to speak to Ryan, and she couldn't *stand* sharp, fussy Grandma. But Elena and Mum were *friends*.

Aunty Elena, Amber and I would catch the 193 bus at quarter to four, which would take us to Lyon's Station, where we would get the five past four train. After that twenty minute train journey, we would then endure a half an hour walk to Mum's flat.

It took me a while to get used to Mum's flat. It didn't

smell right. When we were a family, our home smelt like the comforting combination of washing powder, *Angel Delight* and mum's hairspray. The flat had a damp odour, giving out the impression that it was unlived in. Dad had kept all of the furniture, so Mum had had to buy cheap basic tables and chairs from the market. Our mantelpiece at home was full of frames containing happy shots of the three of us in Portugal, during weekends in Blackpool, on daytrips to Alton Towers. Mum had *one* photo in her flat; my most recent school picture, in a silver frame on the windowsill. It looked so *lonely*. It used to make me cry when I thought of Mum in that flat all by herself.

Please don't tell my mum this, but I really *did* love, love, *love* living with my dad. He had always been the less strict parent, and thrillingly, my bedtime changed from half past eight to nine O'clock! On the days that football was on TV, I was allowed to stay up right until the end of the match, *even* on a school night! We'd watch the game together, sprawled at either end of the sofa with a bag of crisps and a bottle of *Coke* to share. Dad would teach me football phrases and all of the rules of the game. I *even* know what the offside rule is!

My Dad is the *coolest* dad EVER. Loads of my friends complained about their dads, saying they trumped a lot and made bad jokes, or were really bossy. I always felt so lucky whenever I heard any of this; *my* Dad wasn't like that at all. *My* Dad's jokes were hilarious, and he was never, *ever* bossy. He did trump *sometimes*, but even *that* was funny. He could trump the *National Anthem*!

Of course, there *were* times I just *wished* that I could have both of my parents back in the same house again, but I had to think myself very lucky that I still *had* both my mum and dad around. I knew that some children aren't that fortunate.

For anyone whose parents have split up or divorced, just remember it is *not* your fault, and both your Mum and your Dad still love *you* very much.
Sometimes it's better for parents to split up - if they're arguing all the time it causes a lot of stress, not just for them, but for you, too.
If you feel upset about divorce, you should talk to an adult you trust.
I talked to my Uncle Ryan, who explained that just because my parents' didn't love each other anymore, it *didn't* mean that they loved me any less.
Your school teachers, Grandparents and your best friends will also help you.
I found that there were lots of books at the local library all about divorce. Some were fact books about how to deal with it, but others were stories about children going through the *exact* same thing as *I* was. These books really helped me. It made me feel better to know that actually, I *wasn't* alone, and I *could* get through this.
Keep your chin up – things *will* get better, I promise.

Chapter Two -
The People of Deergate

I got to know all of the teachers at Deergate, and most of the pupils. I even knew some of the teacher's first names too, and when I was in a giddy, mischievous mood, I sometimes said, "Thanks, Susan." instead of "Thanks, Mrs Phillips." It always got me into a *lot* of trouble, but it worth it because everyone in the class laughed, and that made me feel good.

My reception teacher was called Mrs Kirkby. I don't remember a great deal about reception, because I was only five years old. However, there is one particular memory that still haunts me, and that is the recollection of the first time I ate the canteen's mash potato. Most of the meals in the canteen were amazing, even *after* Jamie Oliver had banished *Turkey Twizzlers*, but the lumpy, cardboard-tasting mash potato was something I *never* warmed to. The disgusting smell of it swarming the corridors will never leave me.

Mrs Kirkby had a blonde bob and she was *really* fab at playing the guitar. We used to sing a song that went: *'Blue is the colour I like best, from the deep blue sea to the Deergate vest, blue is the colour I like best!'* and she'd strum a calm melody on her guitar.

In year one I had Mrs Beck. She was a glamorous but stern lady who got the best out of her six year old pupils. Mrs Beck had lovely, sloping handwriting that I marvelled at, trying to copy. I remember one parent's evening she told my mum that I was a chatterbox so she had moved me onto a table with the boys in a bid to shut me up. Apparently, this had proven to be even worse, as I showed all the boys my wobbly teeth, and then got into a debate about football with them, chatting *even more* than I had done with the girls!

My year two teacher was Miss Cooks. She was in a good mood the WHOLE year because she was getting married in the summer. I don't remember her shouting once. Her fiancé used to buy her loads of boxes of chocolates, and she often brought them in to share with us. On Valentine's Day, her fiancé sent her a *ginormous* bunch of ruby red roses, which was delivered in the middle of maths! Miss Cooks blushed as red as the roses, *especially* when we all started making kissy noises and chanting '*wit woo!*'

Years three and four were owned by Mrs Walker, whom I also had in year six. She came across as quite no-nonsense and strict, what with her old fashioned skirts and short temper, but really, she was the *best* teacher at Deergate. She took an interest in each pupil, and always came up with the best solutions to any problem and worries.

I had my first male teacher in year five. Mr Helix was funny, and let us read the *Beano*. It seemed he was allergic to maths, and had an obsession with joke books! *And* he was never seen without a cup of coffee... Despite being a man, he was really quite useless with technology. Our class was the first to have an interactive whiteboard fitted, and Mr Helix succeeded in breaking it on the very first day by spilling coffee over it!

Mr Powell was the headmaster of the school, and he was very, *very* scary. Well, he looked very, *very* scary with his 6 foot 3 frame, jet black hair and almost constant frown, but actually, he was really lovely. All four walls of Mr Powell's office were decorated with pictures drawn by his pupils, and his very own children. His desk was full of photos of his wife and his son and daughter. It made him seem a *lot* less intimidating, in my opinion. (I only knew what the inside of Mr Powell's office looked like after being sent there in disgrace for calling Mrs Walker by her first name again. I had been shaking with fear as I was summoned in, but Mr Powell seemed to find the situation quite comical!)

Mrs Kane was the best dinner lady in the *whole history* of dinner ladies! She was a tiny plump lady who wore a red coat every single day, even in the summer. She was the one you went to when you fell over, and no matter how cut your knee was, or how scratched your elbows had gotten, it was nothing one of 'Mrs Kane's magic rubs better' couldn't solve. She was in constant demand; a train of reception children tagging along after her, hanging off her arm every lunch time.

Annabelle and Charlotte were my very *best* friends. Everyone had their own little groups, although we were *all* friends with each other.
Annabelle, Charlotte and I had been total *BFF's* since we were in year three. We got paired up for a Tudor project, and after that we were inseparable, though we *were* totally different.
Annabelle was a girly-girl who wore pigtails every day, fastened with little *Disney Princess* clips. She enjoyed ballet, *loved* anything sparkly and fluffy, and collected pink cuddly toys, which made buying her birthday presents *easy-peasy*.
Charlotte was a chubby, small girl. Whereas Annabelle

was quite tall for her age, Charlotte was the *complete* opposite - when she was ten, she looked about seven. Her cheeks were constantly crimson, her bright blue eyes always shining. Her light brown hair, styled into a bob, hung on either side of her cheeks, making them look chubbier. She worshipped her pony, Buttons, and talked non-stop about how *wonderful* he was. It was torture when it was *her* turn to choose our game at playtimes. She'd almost *always* choose to play horses. We had to cavort after Charlotte, holding onto reins (a skipping rope), shouting *'Canter!'*

I suppose *I* was the tom-boy of the group. I cherished football, and at weekends I went around in tracksuit bottoms and an England football shirt. For special treats, Dad and Uncle Ryan would take me to watch Manchester City play. I *loved* those days. Dad, Uncle Ryan and I would holler out *'Blue Moon'* as we sped along the motorway to the Etihad Stadium. Once there, we'd buy a match day programme and three paper trays brimming with stale chips, and take to our seats. Dad would pick me up, raising me high above his shoulders whenever the Mighty Blues scored.

My bedroom was dedicated to Manchester City: sky blue walls, player posters, and an entire bookshelf full of old match day programmes.

Dad often took me to the local park for a kick about. Dad was always the goalie, and I was the striker. I could quite easily score 2, 3, 4, sometimes even 5 goals in half an hour!

Dad called me his *Little Footy Star*.

I desired to be in a proper girl's team, but there were none in the area.

All of our passions combined, as you can imagine, our Tudor project had some *extremely* interesting results. Charlotte, Annabelle and I decided to dress up as three of Henry V111's six wives. We pretend we were on a *Jeremy Kyle* style show discussing why he had divorced and split up with us, putting our own twist on things.

"I was Henry's first wife, but he said he couldn't be doing with me trying to dye his hair blonde, plait his beard, and take him to my ballet classes, so he chucked me," Annabelle had said, acting as Catherine of Aragon. "To be honest, I'm rather lucky he didn't behead me, but then again, I'm too pretty to behead."

"I'm Anne of Cleaves, his fourth wife, but he divorced me too. He said I spent too much time with the horse that pulled his carriage. He was just jealous because the horse was better looking than him, and it had better teeth," Charlotte piped up.

"And I'm Katherine Parr, Henry's widower," I cried dramatically. "I can't say I'm too bothered about the death of my husband; it's given me more time to play footy in the palace gardens. I only married him for the fame so I could meet a footballer and become a WAG, anyway."

The class loved our project, and so did Mrs Walker. We got a special sticker each and 10 minutes extra break! Despite being such different girls, that project marked the start of our special friendship.

At primary school, no-one really *cared* about what each other looked like.

If someone *was* wearing make-up, nobody would notice.

The boys liked the girls for their personality, not their lip-gloss, and the girls liked the boys for their sense of humour, rather than their hair gel.

My *first* boyfriend was Sid. Of course, he wasn't a *proper* boyfriend - we were only seven - but we *did* write each other love notes and play kissy-cats at break time.

In year six, Aston and I were boyfriend and girlfriend for *two whole months*, and won 'Couple of the Year' in the school playground awards!

I didn't really speak to him out of school, except when I went to the park to play football with him and the other lads during the holidays. Come to think of it, I didn't really talk to him a lot *in* school either, but it was nice to have someone's name to write in the middle of my love hearts pencil case.

Aston was a tall boy with a mop of black hair, and eyes so dark they were almost coal.

I felt *so* grown up telling everybody that I had a *boyfriend.* Mum tutted and said that boys were 'more trouble than they were worth,' whatever *that* meant. Grandma told me I was 'far too young' to have a boyfriend. Uncle Rob roared with laughter. Aunty Elena asked me if Aston was cute. Dad pretended to be cross, and put his hands on his hips, but when he dropped me off at school the following day, he made a point of going right over to Aston and shaking his hand! Dad thought he was being *dead* funny, but I had never seen Aston look so terrified. I was *mega* embarrassed, but that's my Dad for you!

There are plenty of special people at everyone's primary

school, whether it's one of the dinner ladies who knows your mum so always gives you an extra chunk of chocolate brownie, the crying reception child you helped down the stairs on their first day, or even a stray cat you made friends with through the fence on the field.
All of these people are part of your childhood, and you'll probably always remember them.

Cara Jasmine Bradley

Chapter Three -
Our Last Christmas At Deergate

Our last Christmas at Deergate was particularly emotional.

Year six had the fun task of staging our very own version of *The Nutcracker*, and Annabelle was deemed a suitable candidate for the main part.

I was cast as a dancer – with a difference! Our plan was to put a modern spin on the original story, and we all agreed that instead of performing graceful ballet routines, we would dress in the wackiest costumes we could conjure up, and dance around like fools. Annabelle was reluctant to agree to the idea, so Mrs Walker said that she could show off some of her traditional ballet dancing as a contrast, if she liked. Annabelle *did* like.

Rehearsals for our last primary school Christmas play started in mid-November. It was to be performed to the parents on the day we broke up for the Christmas holidays: 23rd December.

I practiced my nonsensical dance so much I could practically do it with my eyes closed.

Dad and I had *tremendous* fun raiding his wardrobe for items of clothing I could wear.

"Gorgeous!" Dad laughed, as I span round in an oversized beige and green striped jumper, and a pair of baggy blue and white pyjama bottoms.

"Positively *stunning*," I agreed, collapsing into Dad, giggling.

Our hard work paid off.

Year six got a standing ovation for our play on that crisp

winter's night.

Looking into the crowd of cheering parents, I felt as though I was in the West End, clasping hands with Annabelle and Charlotte as we took a bow.

The best sight of all was Mum, Dad, Grandma, Uncle Rob, Aunty Elena and Amber all at the very front, clapping, looking so proud of me. Mum and Dad might have been sat as far away from one another as possible, but that didn't matter. They could have sat on the roof for all I cared - they were both there and that was the best thing *ever*.

I stared down at my family and grinned. It was true: they may not love each other anymore, but they certainly loved me a *lot*.

Annabelle's mum was weeping with pride. During the performance, we had spotted her standing up in-between the rows of seats, joining in with all of Annabelle's ballet moves in her skinny jeans and high heels.

Annabelle's Dad's yells were audible above the cheers: "Well done, baby girl!"

Annabelle looked embarrassed, but still leapt off stage to give her Dad a hug.

Charlotte's Mum stood on her chair and took photos of us all, while her Dad whistled and *whooped*. They didn't seem to care that Charlotte has actually fallen off the stage mid performance, while getting a little *too* into her role as a mad dancer!

Mrs Walker took centre stage and made a speech.

"Well as you all know, that was their last Christmas play with us here at Deergate, but they did us proud. Judging by all of the hard work and dedication

that went into that play, I have no doubt that every one of them will succeed at high school. Have a lovely Christmas."
Seeing Mrs Walker in tears made *us* cry.

I had a relaxing Christmas. I spent Christmas Eve day at Mum's, baking mince pies and making paper-chains.
Dad picked me up at half past six, and we went to Uncle Rob's for a feast and movie night.
Dad and Uncle Rob sprawled on the sofa, while Aunty Elena fussed around, making sure Uncle Rob didn't eat all of the crisps, and that there was enough sausage rolls.
Grandma sat stiffly in the armchair, her knitting needles *ching-chinging* with every swift movement.
Amber and I lounged on the floor, watching all of our favourite Christmas movies. I helped Amber write her letter to Santa, which we left with his mince pie, glass of milk, and reindeer carrot by the fireplace.

Amber fell asleep *long* before midnight. Uncle Rob took her up to bed.
I willed my eyes to stay open.
Grandma also fell asleep, but was awoken by Dad's cheering when the clock crept towards Christmas Day.

"Oh for heaven's sake, David! Must you yell so?" She scolded.

"Cheer up you old misery, it's Christmas!" Uncle Rob cried.

"Merry Christmas, Grandma," I said, kissing her leathery cheek.
She chuckled, the lines of annoyance on her face ceasing.

"Merry Christmas to you too, dear."

"Happy Christmas, babe," Aunty Elena

whispered, hugging me.

Uncle Rob grabbed his wife and I, and along with Dad and a reluctant Grandma, we had a group hug. Between them, Dad and Uncle Rob picked Grandma up and gently threw her in the air, catching her a few seconds later. At first, she protested to her sons bitterly, but then even she couldn't help laughing. I demanded a go at being tossed about like a pancake, and got a serious case of the giggles!

I don't know who was more excited about Christmas: me, or Dad and Uncle Rob. The pair of them slung their arms around one another's shoulders, swaying, and belted out a very *terrible* version of East 17's '*Stay Another Day.*'

Aunty Elena had to step in to remind them that we had neighbours to consider when they attempted an encore of '*Santa Baby.*'

Despite not getting home from Uncle Rob's until the early hours of Christmas morning, I still woke at half past seven.

"Dad!" I screamed, running into his room, tugging on my dressing gown. "It's Christmas! *Get up!*"

He mumbled something inaudible about wellington boots, rolling over.

"Come *on* Dad! I want my presents!"

Dad was like a big kid himself when he unwrapped the present that I had bought him - a model of a silver Vauxhall car, just like ours.

He still had a vast collection of toy cars from when he was a boy, and often took them out of their box in the loft to play races with me in the living room.

"I *love* it, Poll! Thank you!"

I loved Dad's present *even more*: a personalised Manchester City shirt!

"Polly: number 10! Thank you Dad, it's just *sooo* cool!"

"I thought you would like it," Dad chuckled. "Open that envelope there. It'll reveal just *why* I bought you that shirt…"

It was only tickets to see Manchester City play Manchester United!

"Oh WOW, oh WOW, OH WOW!" I shrieked, and I ran around the room with my hands in the air in sheer delight, as if *I* had scored a goal.

"I can't wait!" Dad enthused. "Me, you, Uncle Rob, and little Amber. It will Amber's first game at the Etihad - we're bringing her up well. The atmosphere will be brilliant. Now, I'm going to have a shower and get changed. We'll leave for Christmas dinner at Rob's at half past twelve, then I'll drive you up to your Mum's for the evening."

I sat at the foot of the Christmas tree and admired my new gifts.

As well as the shirts and tickets, I had also received a new football, a football computer game, a book full of toilet jokes (I told you my Dad is the best!), and a poster of the current Manchester City squad to add to my collection.

A terrifying realisation hit me, resulting in a pang of fear suddenly catching in my chest.

This time next year, I would be at High School.

How different would things be then?

Would it still be acceptable for me to love football? Or

would I be forced to act all grown-up and girly and lady-
like?
Instead of receiving a beloved City shirt for Christmas,
would I be getting make-up?
The thought of this petrified me. I didn't *want* to change
- I was happy as I was.
And now there were only seven months left at
Deergate…

Chapter Four -
To Grow Up Or Not To Grow Up,
That Is The Question?

I started to get very nostalgic in the New Year.
All that went through my mind was: *'This is my last
January at Deergate.'* and *'It's snowing - is this the last
time I'll see Deergate in the snow?'*
I questioned Annabelle and Charlotte on the situation.

"Annabelle, Charlotte... Are you scared about
high school?" I asked one lunch time.

"Nah, nothing to worry about," Charlotte replied
casually.

"No, I can't *wait!*" Annabelle enthused.

"But, like... What about having to wear make-up,
and things like that?"

"Hmm, I don't mind. Might make me look a bit
older," Charlotte sighed.

"I *always* wear make-up," Annabelle simpered.
"My Daddy bought me a beauty case for Christmas and
I'm allowed to wear pink glittery eye shadow for ballet."

The fear of high school *constantly* played on my
mind. It felt like whatever I did, there was always an
unresolved issue lurking in my head. The time seemed to
suppress me, and for the first time ever - to my absolute
dismay - the weeks started to fly by. I didn't *want* to
leave my beloved primary school. *I wasn't ready to grow
up.*
I'd always enjoyed school, but the knowledge that I was
about to lose it gave me a new appreciation for it.
Everything about primary school was just so cosy, so
comfortable, so... *Normal.* The routine of day to day life

was one which I had been doing for seven years, and
having that familiarisation snatched away from me
before I was ready made me want to cry.

From Grandma's window, I watched the high school
students get off their bus at the stop across the road. They
yelled and jostled each other, shoving and barging.
I recognised one girl, Leonie Armitage. She was in the
year above me and had left Deergate a year ago to go to
the high school. I remembered her as a quiet, meek girl
with bunches and a passion for basketball. Looking at her
now, it looked as if basketball was the least of her
passions.
The bunches had been replaced by a stylish haircut and a
quirky side fringe. She was no longer wearing the custom
Deergate bright blue jumper, grey knee-length skirt, and
white lacy ankle socks. She was now dressed in a sharp
navy blazer, which flapped open as she walked to reveal
a crisp white shirt and a blue and yellow tie. Her blue
pleated skirt had been hitched way above her knees,
where her socks had been pulled up to.
From across the road, I could see that she was wearing
lots of smudged eye make-up.
I sunk back from the window, horrified. I blinked back
confused tears.
I didn't *want* to change! Why did I have to leave lovely
little Deergate?

No sooner had I got my head around the fact that it was
January, it suddenly turned into February.
On Valentine's Day, Aston left a packet of heart shaped
sweets under my literacy book in my drawer. I wondered

if we'd still be boyfriend and girlfriend this time *next* year. He would probably find a prettier girl at high school; one that wore make-up like Leonie.

At Mum's one Friday night, I excused myself from the table and crept into her room.
Now, *where* did she keep her make-up? Ah yes, in a small flowery bag on the dressing table.
I stared at myself in the mirror. I was quite pale. My light brown hair was scraped back into its usual low ponytail. My best feature was probably my brown eyes, outlined with long black eyelashes.
With a shaking hand, I slowly pulled back the zip of mum's make-up bag, gingerly inspecting the contents.
I smeared an orange liquid over my cheeks. That certainly added colour, although not a very nice one.
Applying mascara was a challenge. I'd watched Mum do her's numerous times, and I'd once put some *pink* mascara on at Annabelle's for a laugh, but this time, my hand was so unsteady I just couldn't get it right. I couldn't help but blink when I moved the brush near my eyelid. The wand jabbed my eyeball by accident, and in a shocked flurry of eyelashes, the substance smudged all over my face. Tutting, I blended it in, hoping it would look like eyeliner.
The sharp point of Mum's startling red lipstick frightened me, and it looked very out of place on my face.
As a final touch, I used a big, tickly brush to dab a pink powdery thing onto each of my cheeks.
Frowning at my new reflection, I realised that I didn't exactly look dissimilar to a clown I had seen at the circus

Dad had taken me to a few weeks ago. Make-up hadn't looked good on him, and it *certainly* didn't look good on me.

Is this what you had to look like when you left primary school?

"Polly? What are you doing, angel?"
Mum appeared at the doorway behind me.
I turned round. She looked shocked.

"What on earth have you done to yourself, you silly girl? I hope that's not my best lipstick you're wearing! Honestly Polly, what *do* you look like?!"

"I don't know. *I* don't like it either." I burst into tears.

"Poll? What *is* the matter?" Mum's angry tone softened. She knelt on the floor in front of me. "All that mascara is running down your face!"
I rubbed the back of my hand angrily across my cheeks. When I looked down at my hands, they were covered in a streaky black residue.

"Come on, into the bathroom. We'll have this off in no time."
Mum had a packet of special wipes to remove make-up, and in less than five minutes, three of them were a blur of orange, black, and red from my face.

"There – as good as new." Mum smiled, turning me round to look in the mirror.
My face was back to its old self; reassuring, comforting.

"I can't understand it though... You don't *like* make-up. Why did you want to try mine?"

"Because... Because-" I stammered, trying to blink back fresh tears. How could I *ever* even begin to explain to anyone how I was feeling? "Because I'm going to have to start wearing make-up in September when I get to high school, so I was just testing to see how I look, and I look *horrid*! I don't *want* to go to high school, I want to stay at Deergate! I don't *want* to wear make-up and short skirts and be all girly and grown up - I just want to be *me*!"

Mum stared at me for a few seconds, then pulled me close into a warm hug.

"Oh, Polly. Don't you worry yourself anymore, doll. You're beautiful as you are. You don't need to change just because you start high school - you don't have to change *at all*. *You* choose when you want to wear make-up; it might be next month, it might be never. Don't be in any hurry to grow up, because childhood is very precious. It goes so fast - you should try and preserve it as long as you can, babe. Besides – you'll be nearly 12 when you start high school, and 12 years old is *not* a grown up! Wait until you're my age!"

"But I saw Leonie the other day and she had make-up on, and Annabelle wears it already, but I don't *want* to," I sobbed.

"Then don't. There's no rule anywhere that states that you have to start wearing make-up as soon as you go to high school. Leonie and Annabelle wear make-up because they want to, and that's totally fine, too. But *you* don't have to. You don't change as a person just because you change schools, you know!"

I sniffed. "Really?"

"Really. Have I changed since I moved house?"

"No."

"Exactly! Our circumstances might change in life, but that doesn't mean we change as people. Not unless

we want to. You carry on being you, Poll, because you're my amazing, clever, beautiful, funny daughter, and I wouldn't change you for the world! Now, do you fancy some ice-cream and a movie marathon?"
Did I!

As I sat on the sofa with Mum, two spoons in the cookie dough ice-cream, watching one of my favourite movies, I suddenly felt as though a weight had been lifted off my shoulders. Just speaking to Mum about my fears and listening to her perspective and logic had made me feel a *million* times better.
Mum had definitely put a stop to certain worries, but she couldn't end the sadness that had become part of my life: the sadness that I would be leaving Deergate very soon…

Chapter Five - Chesterlanes High School

July came quicker than I ever imagined it would.
January, February, March, April, May and June passed in a blur of Manchester City matches, kick abouts in the park with Dad, shy, awkward trips to the sweet shop with Aston, sleepovers with Charlotte and Annabelle, and the constant reminder that this time next year, things would all be *very* different.

July promised to be a busy month: as well as our intense SATs revision, we also had a day trip to the high school, our leaver's disco, AND rehearsals for our 'leaver's assembly,' which was to be performed at the end of the month.

Mrs Walker was at the end of her tether.
Mr Helix was apparently neglecting the national curriculum once again; seemingly more interested in teaching his class all of the verses to '(*Is This the Way To) Amarillo?*'
His classroom was next to ours, and the constant out-of-tune singing proved a *massive* distraction to our revision.
One afternoon, Mrs Walker snapped. She told us to put down our pencils and follow her out of the classroom.
Exchanging baffled looks, we did as we were told. She had us line up outside Mr Helix's classroom, and then instructed us to sing *'(Is This The Way To) Amarillo?'* in our worst, most tuneless voices, as loud as we could.
It was the most bizarre incident, but by far one of the *funniest* moments of my life! I had never seen Mr Helix look so shocked.
Mrs Walker stood grinning at us proudly as we warbled

through the whole song. Teachers from the other classes came out of their rooms to see what was occurring, bemused and confused looks on their faces.
Needless to say, it was a while before Mr Helix 'blessed us' with his singing again!

I had been absolutely *dreading* the 20th July ever since I had heard what was going to happen that day.
I found it *impossible* to sleep on the night of 19th July. I kicked my quilt off, feeling apprehensive and frustrated at a lack of sleep. The room was too light, too hot. Five minutes without the duvet, and I felt cold and shivery. I yanked it back over me, trying in vain to get comfortable. I tossed and turned every few seconds.
My alarm clock flashed at the hour: eleven O'clock. I had gone to bed two hours ago - *why* couldn't I sleep? After another restless hour, I stood up on my bed and reached for my soft toy shelf. I studied each outline, until my hands discovered the toy I was looking for. Relieved, I stroked the soft, matted fur of the sky blue teddy bear, my hands tracing Manchester City's badge on the front of his stomach. Dad had bought me Moonie at my first City match when I had been just three. Since then, he had been my lucky mascot and my comforter.
I lay down, my arms wrapped around Moonie, and eventually fell asleep, breathing in his musty, soothing smell.

"Poll? Polly, time to get up."
Groggily, I blinked my eyes several times.
"Aww, you've got Moonie there with you!"
Dad stood at my bedroom door.

"Dad? Wh- What time is it?" I muttered.

"Seven."

"I get up at eight," I mumbled, confused.

"Not today you don't - it's your taster day at the high school. You've got to get the bus at eight."

I groaned. The dreadful day had finally arrived.

Dad made me pancakes for breakfast, smearing generous amounts of chocolate spread on them. Usually, I would have greatly appreciated this offering, but it was all I could do to manage a mere mouthful today.

"Don't worry Poll, it'll be fine," Dad said reassuringly, as if he could read my mind.

Would it be fine? I didn't think so. Today was the day I would find out the truth: what high school was *really* like. I would get an idea of how different things were there. And I had a horrible feeling I wasn't going to like it...

Charlotte and Annabelle came to call for me at twenty to eight.

Dad answered the door.

"Hello, you two. Gosh, you're early! The bus stop is only five minutes away - what have you set out this early for?"

"We didn't want to be late," Charlotte replied.

"Ah, I see. Well it looks like you're in good time. Come on Polly, time to get going."

I swung my rucksack over my shoulders and made my way to the door, giving my best friends a wan smile.

We didn't speak much on the walk through the avenues into the village. Even Annabelle was unusually quiet.

The bus stop was crowded with scary teenagers in navy

blazers.

A huddle of anxious faces in bright blue jumpers gave Charlotte, Annabelle and I a clue as to where the rest of our classmates were.

Mrs Walker had come to the bus stop to wave us off. All of Deergate's year sixes crowded around her.

"You all look terrified!" She laughed. "It's going to be absolutely fine. The bus journey should take about half an hour, and then one of the teachers will meet you at the other end. Stick together, have lots of fun, and I'll see you all back at Deergate tomorrow."

Poor Annabelle had to sit on her own on the bus. Charlotte bagged the seat next to me, leaving her to sit opposite us.

The boys made straight for the back of the bus, shoving each other, but they retreated back down to the front when the older lads from the high school declared the back '*Theirs.*'

Aston gave me an anxious smile as he walked past me. The older boys started setting fire to their own trumps and chanting silly things at the girls. I cast a glance over at Annabelle, who was not usually a shrinking violet when it came to boys. She was staring straight ahead, her eyes wide.

I didn't even speak to Charlotte on the journey. I stared out of the window, willing the coach to break down, or *anything* that would prevent us from getting to our destination. To my horror, within seemingly no time at all, the bus pulled through a pair of wrought iron gates, and it was then that we got our first view of Chesterlanes High School.

It was an ugly building. At first glance, I thought the bus

had taken a wrong turning at a prison. The concrete jungle playground was dreary, and lacked hopscotch paintings and pots of brightly coloured flowers. A tall metal fence ran round the perimeter of the school. Gangs of older boys stood around at the entrance, their uniforms scruffy, glaring up at the buses as they passed.

If it hadn't been for the plump, kindly looking lady who met us off the bus, I think I might have burst into tears then and there.

"Deergate Primary School? Follow me. I'll take you to the hall where you can meet the year sixes from the other schools. I'm Mrs Bobby, and I'll be looking after you today. "

Charlotte, Annabelle and I linked arms.

All around us, older kids shouted and *whooped* and barged.

The atmosphere was so different to how it was at Deergate. Here, it was intense, serious and scary. At Deergate, it was easy, comfy, and laid-back.

We were used to being the oldest pupils at Deergate, but here, at Chesterlanes High School, we were the babies again.

We were shown into the hall – a menacing dark room with a sea of plastic blue chairs stretching from front to back. Equally anxious faces stared back at us in different coloured jumpers from the chairs: the year sixes from the other primary schools. There were about 200 eleven year olds in the hall. I took a strange comfort in knowing that every single person in the room would be feeling as nervous as I was.

It was already shaping up to be very different to how assemblies at primary school were taken. At Deergate, we all filed into the little hall to the sound of Heather Small's inspirational song '*Proud*' drifting from the CD player. Today, we tiptoed into the vast space to the sound of teenage boys shouting and swearing from the corridors, teachers yelling "DETENTION - LUNCH TIME!" after them.

A tall, slim man with a smart suit and black rimmed glasses took to the front of the hall and cleared his throat.

"Welcome to Chesterlanes High School. My name is Mr Pontin and I am going to be your Head of Year. It will seem very scary at first, but trust me, you will get used to it. High school is very different to primary school, but it has its advantages. Today, you will be given a tour of the school and have the opportunity to sample a few lessons. I hope you enjoy your day here, and I look forward to seeing you all in September."

There was a brief second of silence, which was shattered by a burst of chatter from every corner of the room.

"What do we do now?" Charlotte hissed.

"How should I know?" Annabelle snapped.

I sat there in silence, staring straight ahead. *I was so nervous.*

In a flourish of light pink cardigan, beige skirt and pearls, Mrs Bobby strode to the front of the hall.

"You will now be sorted into groups of 30 for your tours. If you aren't with anyone you know, *don't panic.* You will soon make new friends - this is what today is all about."

Agonisingly, we were forced to sit in apprehensive silence while every single person in the hall had their name read out, and the designated groups were formed. To my horror, I wasn't with Charlotte *or* Annabelle. In fact, the only people I was familiar with in my group were two rowdy boys from Deergate. I sidled closer to them, but they were seemingly feeling over-confident to be in one another's company and sauntered away from me.

I was left to walk on my own, at the back of the huddle.

The leader of my group introduced herself as Miss Fallows, a biology teacher. She was very small and slight, looking as if she herself should be wearing a primary school uniform. Her wispy, mouse hair fell like dainty curtains on either side of her heart shaped face. Miss Fallows wore glasses, but no make-up. She spoke with a quiet, shy voice, pushing her glasses up her nose ever so often.

"As I am a science teacher, I shall first show you the laboratories."

Laboratories? At Deergate, we did science sat at our tables, often involving batteries and bulbs, and nothing more.

"Science at high school is very different from science at primary school," Miss Fallows said, as if to read my thoughts. "Come September, long gone will be the days of hooking up bulbs to create a circuit! You will discover many more interesting experiments, such as crystal growing."

Annabelle would like that.

The laboratories *were* impressive. Wooden benches stretched across each room, laden with mysterious looking scientific equipment. Bright blue aprons hung on the back of the doors, safety goggles below them.

The maths and English rooms were similar to our primary school classrooms, except there were a lot more

of them on either side of seemingly endless corridors.
I peered in through the windows of the musty
classrooms. Accusing faces of older children glowered
back at me, disturbed from their work.
Miss Fallows led us on through the school.

"On to the Physical Education department. We
have lots of clubs available in this department:
basketball, cheerleading, tennis, football..."
Football? Well, it would just be a boy's team, *wouldn't*
it?

"... We even have a *girl's* football team," Miss
Fallows concluded.
I looked up.
Wow, oh wow! A *real* girl's team!

"Does the girl's team get to play in proper
matches?" I piped up, edging forwards.

"They sure do! They travel all around the area for
tournaments. In fact, we Chesterlanes Girls have been
crowned regional champions this season," Miss Fallows
replied.
I grinned, despite myself. Suddenly, high school didn't
seem *quite* so bad...

We were shown the food technology department
next.
At Deergate, we did cookery once a year, if that. At
Chesterlanes, we were expected to have one lesson a
week!

"I believe over the course of year seven, you will
all be making fruit salads, pasties, burgers, flapjacks,
muffins, and macaroni cheese. Each week, you will be
asked to supply your own ingredients, and you can take
your bakes home for your family to try," explained Miss

Fallows.

We were allowed five minutes free time to explore the kitchens. I hung back from the group again, my shyness taking hold.

A tall girl, her black hair pulled into a high ponytail and fastened with a big, floral bobble, hung back with me. She was kitted out in a red jumper and black skirt, which I recognised to be the uniform of the primary school in the next village.

I sneakily cast a look at her. She looked at me. We caught each other's eye and smiled timidly.

"I'm Francesca. So, you like football too then?"

"Hi, I'm Polly. Yes, I *love* it! I play *all the time* at the park with my Dad, but I've never played on a *proper* team before. I'd like to join the team here in September. I want to be a professional lady footballer when I'm older," I burbled. I suddenly stopped, aware that I was going on a bit. I blushed, feeling rude. "Do *you* like football?"

"I *love* football!" Francesca exclaimed. "I want to play professionally when I'm older, too."

"Are you on a team at the moment?"

"No, there's nothing round here for girls, is there? I usually play with my older brothers at the park. Well, when they can be bothered, that is. You're so lucky that your Dad plays football with you - mine is too busy with his boring old car, or the garden."

"Oh, that's rubbish. My Dad is *amazing*. I think he was a bit disappointed when he discovered I was a girl when I was born, but I bet he's glad now! All I talk about is football, and he doesn't half encourage me."

"Wow, that sounds brilliant! Perhaps I could

come to the park with you one day? Which one do you go to?"

"The one in Deergate Village - the big playing fields by the shops."

"My Grandma and Grandad live opposite there! We can meet up over the summer. Well... If you'd like to?"

"That would be great!" I cried.

We were joined by the rest of the group, babbling excitedly about food technology lessons.

"Ok folks, lunch time! You've got an hour. Follow the signs along the corridor for the canteen, and take your pick of the meals. Meet back here at one O'clock," Miss Fallows instructed.

"Mind if I walk down to the canteen with you?" Francesca asked.

"Of course not. I was so scared I wouldn't make any friends today. Looks like I've already proved myself wrong there. *And* you like football, which is a friendship bonus!"

The canteen was rapidly filling up with a sea of multicoloured jumpers.

Francesca and I stood in the doorway, taking in the mass of colour and the appetising smells that greeted us.

"My friends are over there," Francesca said, pointing out a group of lads in red jumpers. "Mind if I go and sit with them? I'll meet you back at one, Polly."

I met up with Annabelle while queuing for pasta and cheese.

"Polly! I've missed you," she said. "Had a good morning?"

"I've missed you too. Yes thanks, have you?"

"Yes, I have. Have you *seen* the dance studio? I just *know* I'm going to *love* it here. I'll be dancing like Beyonce by year eight! Oh, and I can't *wait* to do textiles. Apparently, you get to make bags! My designs might get spotted by *Vogue*! *And* I've made friends with a *really* cute boy."

Charlotte joined us at twenty past twelve.

"Where have *you* been?" Annabelle demanded.

"I got chatting to my group leader. She's called Mrs Willis - teaches English. She's got a horse called Sparky. She said she'll bring in some photos of him in September to show me."

None of us were reluctant to head back to our groups at one O'clock.

The afternoon was peacefully dedicated to playing games in an abandoned Spanish classroom.

"Right, just so we can get to know each other a little better, I want one person to start off by saying their name, and two interesting facts about themselves. They'll then pick someone else in the room, who will go next. We will carry on until everyone has had a go," Miss Fallows said.

"My name is Jensen. I like sport, and I have a Boxer dog called Rufus."

Jensen, a good looking boy with a head of brown hair and freckles, pointed in my direction.

"*Me*?" Questioned everyone around me, confused.

"The girl with the blue jumper and brown hair," Jensen clarified, pointing straight at me.

"Oh... I'm Polly. I love football, and I have the

cutest cousin ever, called Amber."

I tried to memorise everybody's name as we went around the room, but the only two I could remember were those of Francesca and Jensen. One thing was for certain though - everyone looked as young as I did. None of the girls were wearing make-up, nor did they look like they had any intentions of starting to cake their faces in it any time soon. For the first time in months, I suddenly felt very relaxed.

After a few hours, a shrill, startling noise sounded throughout the school.

We all jumped.

"Aw, bless you all, jumping out of your skin," Miss Fallows laughed. "That was the bell marking the end of the day - you're free! Thank you very much for today, it has been a pleasure meeting you all, and I look forward to teaching some of you in September. Make your way up to the buses, and have a safe journey home."

In the sudden rush of people surging for the door, I linked my arm through Francesca's.

We followed the crowd to the row of buses at the top of the school, and sought out the rest of our primary school classmates.

"My bus is here," Francesca said. "What's your number, Polly? I'll ring you to arrange our football match."

I scribbled my number on a piece of paper torn out of my notebook and handed it to her, hastily waving goodbye and running for my own bus.

Chapter Six -
The Leaver's Disco

After our successful day at Chesterlanes, everyone was
thoroughly looking forward to high school. I felt a lot
more laid-back about the whole situation now that I knew
it was nothing to fear. High school promised many new
opportunities, and I was itching to get myself onto that
girl's football team!
The only thing to overcome now was the sadness that
lingered in my mind whenever I thought of leaving
Deergate forever.

Our last week at Deergate pounced on us unexpectedly.
Year six had gone very fast. *Too fast.*
Before I knew it, I was running home after our last
Thursday to get myself ready for the Leaver's Disco,
which was being held in the school hall at half past six
that night.
 I'd been shopping with Mum on Saturday. Even *I*
had agreed that wearing my football kit to the disco was
much too informal, so had agreed to hit the town with
Mum, who had promised to buy me any outfit I wanted
from the fashion shops.
I couldn't have been less interested in fashion had I tried,
but I accepted Mum's offer as graciously as I could.
Annabelle had bought her disco outfit *months* ago, and
Charlotte and I had been reminded of this every day
since. In fact, Annabelle had talked about it that much,
we could practically conjure up the pink and white
sequined frilly dress in mid-air through sheer
imagination.

Dresses were out of the question for me - I could never figure out what was the right length. Past my knees was too long and made me look like a six year old at a wedding. *Above* my knees was too short, and made me look as if I was off out clubbing. It was hard to find a dress that sat comfortably *on* my knees.

Even Charlotte had bought her outfit. I thought denim shorts, a green smock top and a grey cardigan sounded very glamorous for Charlotte, who was rarely seen out of her horse riding clothes.

I didn't like shorts unless they were printed with the Manchester City logo. I couldn't even imagine wearing denim shorts.

What *was* I going to wear?

I tried on a few pairs of jeans in town, but none of them seemed to suit me.

"How about a nice skirt?" Mum suggested.

I wrinkled my nose. A skirt? I only ever wore a skirt for school. I shrugged.

"You wait there, I've found the perfect outfit for you, Poll." With a flaunt of sweet perfume and a jangle of bangles, Mum swept out of the changing rooms.

She returned a good five minutes later.

"Here, try this on, babe. Show me when you've got it on, yeah?"

Reluctantly, I drew the changing room curtains shut and inspected the outfit she'd selected. A black pleated skirt, a strappy sky blue top, and a black cardigan.

I grimaced at how girly the skirt looked, but the top was the *exact* colour of Manchester City's kit.

Surprisingly, I liked how the outfit looked on me. I stood staring at my reflection in the mirrors, turning this way and that. The skirt sat exactly at my kneecaps.

"Polly? Are you done in there?" Mum called.

Bashfully, I pulled back the curtain.

Mum gasped.

"Oh Polly! You look beautiful! That *really* suits you. Do *you* like it?"

"Yes," I whispered shyly. "I do."

Mum had bought me the outfit and also a pair of plain, flat black shoes. She'd tried to treat me to some silver bangles and a necklace, but I'd insisted that jewellery was a step too far, and asked if I could have the latest footy magazine instead.

When I returned home from school on Thursday, Dad, Aunty Elena, Uncle Rob, Amber, Grandma, and even Mum were sat in the living room waiting for me.

"Hello, party girl!" Dad cheered. "We've got the whole family round to watch you go off to your first disco."

"*Dad*," I groaned. "It's *not* my first disco, I've been to *tonnes* of discos at Deergate."

"Ah, but this is different. This is the end of something."

"And the start of something new," Aunty Elena added, smiling.

"I... I'm not sure I want the old thing to end," I croaked.

"Well you've got one more day to enjoy it then," Grandma replied curtly.

I swallowed. I didn't even want to think about tomorrow. *My last day at Deergate.*

"Come on petal, your Mum and I have come to

style your hair," Aunty Elena said.

"Why? I was just going to tie it back, like I normally do."

"Nonsense! We're going to curl it to perfection," Mum chirped, making curling motions with her fingers.

"Um, alright," I said flatly. "I'm just going to get a shower then."

I sloped upstairs.

Why wasn't I excited for the disco? I usually loved discos. We had two a year at Deergate, and they usually involved lots of sweets, fake tattoos, ridiculous dancing, and a mad DJ playing old cheesy pop songs like '*Black Magic*' and '*Gangnam Style.*'

This one was going to be different, though. This would end a fantastic seven years at a wonderful school. Dad was right, it *was* marking the end of something - something I wasn't ready to leave behind.

The shower hid my tears.

"Have you got a cold coming on, Poll?" Mum enquired when she came up to dry my hair. "You sound all sniffly."

"Maybe," I lied.

"Tough luck, right before the summer holidays, too. You probably caught it off Amber," Aunty Elena said.

"*Mmmmm.*"

I was thankful for the loud, consistent noise of the hairdryer. It meant I didn't have to talk.

"Right, pop your outfit on, then we can start styling your hair," Mum said.

"*Ohhh* yes, I'm *dying* to see this outfit!" Aunty Elena enthused.

I wasn't in the mood for showing off. I wasn't in the mood to act happy and twirl round and have my photo taken.

"*Wow, Polly!*" Aunty Elena screamed as I slunk back into the bedroom in my skirt.

Mum grinned triumphantly. "Doesn't she look gorgeous, Elena?"

"She most certainly does. What a change from football shirts, eh? Honestly, I wish Rob wouldn't dress Amber in that disgusting Manchester City kit. He doesn't seem to realise he has a daughter. I mean, I hate to still be moaning about this, but missing the birth of his daughter because he was at City's cup final? Sometimes I wonder why I bother."

I wished I *was* wearing my football shirt. I'd sooner be playing football at the park with Dad.

Mum and Aunty Elena set to work on my hair, scrunching sections on top of my head and securing them with big clips.

Mum sprayed my locks with an anti-heat product. Aunty Elena began to entwine strands of my thin hair around the curling tongues.

"How long is this going to take?" I groaned.

"It'll take as long as it takes."

"*But Mum*, Annabelle and Charlotte and coming to call for me at quarter past."

"Well that still gives us twenty-five minutes."

Eventually, my hair was finished. It looked weird. I rarely wore it down, but now it cascaded around my shoulders in ringlets.

"What do you think, babe?" Mum quizzed, bending down so that her head was on my shoulder.

"Hmm, it's *okay*," I said.

"Only okay?"

"It's nice," I replied feebly, forcing a smile.

"Aw, she's just shy," Aunty Elena cooed. "I think it looks lush, Poll."

"Doesn't it just, Elena? Right Polly, let's go downstairs and show the others."

I was prodded down the stairs, and tripped awkwardly into the living room.

"Wow, check you out," Uncle Rob said.

"Very nice, Polly. You look like a lady for once," Grandma commented.

Amber blinked at me with big, brown eyes, the dainty curves of her lips pressed into an 'O.'

Dad stayed silent, staring at me.

"Photo time!" Aunty Elena cried. "Stand by the window. Strike a pose!"

I smiled weakly as I had my photo taken with each member of family, then lots on my own.

"Oh, five past six, your friends will be here soon," Mum said.

"Yeah," I muttered. "I just need to get something from upstairs."

It was all I could do not to cry as I shut my bedroom door behind me.

Shaking, I sat down on my bed.

There came a knock at the door. Dad appeared.

"You okay, Poll?"

I nodded. He came into the room, closing the door.

"Dad, I'm really, really scared," I whispered. "I don't want to leave Deergate. This is too weird."

Dad sat down next to me on the bed. "I know. It's weird

70

for me, too. I can't believe that my baby will be at high school in a few months."

"I'm *not* a baby," I sighed.

"You're *my* baby. You always will be, no matter how old you are. You've grown up so much. I can't quite believe it. You look even more beautiful than usual tonight."

"No I don't. I don't like my hair down. And I don't go a bundle on skirts either."

"Well, if I'm honest, I think I prefer you wearing your football shirt and trackie bottoms. *That's* my Polly - my little footy star."

"Can we play football this weekend, Dad?" I asked.

"We can play football every weekend for the rest of our lives, if that's what you'd like," Dad replied. "Just do me a favour, please?"

"What?"

"I want you to enjoy yourself tonight. I want you to forget that you're leaving Deergate tomorrow, and pretend this is just a normal disco. Don't let *anything* ruin your night, okay?"

"Okay Dad. I'll do it for you."

"That's my girl. Now, get on your dancing shoes, sing your heart out to '*Shout Out To My Ex,*' eat loads of sweets, and drink lots of fizzy pop! My, I wish *I* was off to a school disco tonight!"

There was a knock on the front door as I hugged Dad. I heard the key turn in the lock, and then Charlotte's voice asking if I was ready.

I bolted downstairs.

"Here she is! Time for one more picture. Girls,

stand together on the garden path," Mum ordered.

"Oh, not *more* pictures," Charlotte protested. "My Mum has already taken *billions*."

"*And* mine, but I *like* having my photo taken," Annabelle contributed.

I was more than relieved when we were finally on our way up to Deergate.

"I can't walk in these shoes!" Annabelle moaned, stumbling in her black high heels.

"Shouldn't have worn them then," Charlotte replied. She herself was wearing trainers.

"You look really nice, Charlotte," I complimented. "So do you, Annabelle."
Secretly, I thought Annabelle had dressed up a bit *too* much. Her famous dress was a little on the short side, and her glittery eye makeup made her expression appear constantly startled.
Charlotte really *did* look lovely.

"Thanks Polly. You look fab, too. I like your hair like that."

"Yeah, it's nice actually. Not as nice as mine, though," Annabelle giggled. She ran her fingers through her slink, newly straightened hair.

Everyone at the disco looked brilliant. The girls were dressed similar to Charlotte and I, casual but glamorous. The boys had gelled up their hair and were sporting checked shirts and jeans.
Aston gave me a shy wave when I entered the hall. He was looking cute in a green shirt, tucked into his jeans. He had already managed to scuff the knees of his jeans by skidding across the hall floor with the other boys.

The hall had been transformed into a dance floor.

Disco lights hung from the roof, creating millions of multicoloured shapes scurrying about at our feet.
A table of food had been set out along one side, stacked high with paper plates, paper cups, and bottles of pop.
The DJ was in the far corner, blasting out songs which had come out over the past seven years.

I danced with Charlotte, I danced with Annabelle (who had wisely taken off her high heels), I danced with Aston, and I *even* had a quick dance with Mrs Walker.
Mrs Walker was wearing a long, black dress, and was the only person dressed as remotely glamorous as Annabelle, though even she was wearing less make-up.
Annabelle came into her own when '*Barbie Girl*' was played. She knew all the words.
Charlotte and I had more fun embarking upon a sing-off to One Direction's '*You Don't Know You're Beautiful,*' pointing to each other in the chorus and getting a serious case of the giggles.
All three of us indulged in a fake tattoo for old time's sake, done at a table by one of the parents.
The boys all bought those gooey alien pods as they had done each year previously.

Before I knew it, it was nine O'clock, and the first of the parents arrived to collect their year six child.
I was expecting the whole of the Hendrix family clan to turn up and collect me, but I was pleasantly surprised when Dad appeared on his own.
He got chatting to Charlotte's Dad while we finished off our pick and mix and had a chat with Mrs Walker.

"You both look very grown-up tonight, girls," she stated.

"Thank you," I replied.

73

"Thanks, so do you," Charlotte replied, making us all chuckle.

"Annabelle looks grown-up in the extreme," Mrs Walker sighed.

She had already left with her mum, who wanted to be home in time to watch the second half of *Coronation Street*.

"Hmmm," Charlotte agreed.

"I wish you wouldn't grow up so fast. You've got the rest of your lives to grow up, why do you seem so adamant to do it at eleven?"

"*I* don't. I'm in no rush, I like being me. No-one is going to change me."

"I'm very glad to hear that, Polly. You're a lovely girl."

"*I'm* not going to grow up either, Mrs Walker," Charlotte chipped in. "If I grow up, I might outgrow Buttons, then I'd have to sell him, and I would hate, hate, *hate* that."

Mrs Walker laughed; a soft, comforting sound. "Oh, Charlotte. You and that pony! Do you remember when you brought him in for Pet Day in year three? Then there was the time in year four when you came in your riding clothes to non-uniform day."

We giggled, Charlotte going pinker than usual.

"Well, I suppose I'd better let you get off home. It's your last day at Deergate tomorrow! Gosh, I'm not sure if my tears will hold this time."

The sadness that had magically vanished for the disco reappeared with a sharp stab.

I wasn't sure if *my* tears would hold, either.

Chapter Seven -
Our Last Day At Deergate Primary School

The tears came almost as soon as I had woken up the next morning.

I glanced at my Manchester City calendar above my bed, willing the date to be anything *but* the 29th July. Every other day before the 29th had been crossed off. A black ring circled the dreaded date, etched with the sickeningly real words: **Last Day at Deergate**.

Shaking, I pulled on my white polo shirt, grey skirt and blue jumper for the very last time.

I savoured the sweet, primary school smell lingering on my jumper as I pulled it over my head.

I wiped at my tears with the faded blue sleeve.

I didn't have to pretend to Dad. He knew *exactly* how I'd be feeling.

"Hey, Poll. I know you probably won't feel like eating, but try one of these pancakes. Jam, or chocolate spread?"

The jam tasted too sickly, the pancake too dry. I gulped at my glass of water appreciatively, then felt sick.

I thought I *was* going to be sick when I brushed my teeth. I splashed cold water at my face in an attempt to calm me down, but it went in my eye and I spent the next five minutes rubbing it with a towel. When I pulled the towel away, my eye appeared all red and swollen.

My hair wouldn't tame into its usual ponytail because it was still curly from the disco the night before. It stuck out at odd angles, refusing to be brushed through.

I wet my brush and frantically dragged it through my hair, then snapped a bobble around it.

Despite my hectic morning, I was ready with plenty of time to spare before Charlotte and Annabelle came to call for me at quarter to nine.

While Dad had his wash, I sat on the very edge of the sofa, hands clasped in-between my knees.

The rain trickled down the windowpane outside.

Seven years and this was it. Over.

I turned the television on. There wasn't much on, just some kid's show that I'd watched in reception.

Reception. What I wouldn't give to be back there.

I turned the television off.

The magazine rack contained a pile of old Manchester City programmes, which I sifted through. Picking one out, I studied the date on the front. I'd have been in year three then.

I flung it back down and picked out another. I would have been in year five. Sighing, I pushed the magazine rack from sight.

Looking around the room, I glanced at the pictures on the walls. One of me as a fat baby, sitting in a highchair, smearing jam across my face. Another of me holding Amber days after her birth, her miniscule pink fingers clasped around my pale hand.

I *wished* I could go back to those times. I could hardly bring myself to look at the frame in the middle of the mantelpiece, depicting a photo of me at my very first day at Deergate. My hair was in plaits, my skirt far too long, my jumper too baggy. From what I could remember, I had been very nervous that day, too, but oh, how I wished I could go back.

I leapt up from the sofa as soon as I heard the first knock on the front door.

"Bye Dad!" I yelled, flinging the door open.

"Eh? Wait a minute, Polly!" Dad lumbered out of the bathroom, towel draped round his neck, shaving foam covering his face. "Let me have one more photo, of you on your last day."

"Okay," I sighed.

Obviously, *'one more photo'* turned into a few more, and Charlotte, Annabelle and I had to run to school to get there in time.

It was a strange atmosphere inside Deergate Primary School.

Anyone who wasn't in year six was in high spirits at the prospect of the summer holidays starting that afternoon. Everyone that *was* in year six was misty eyed and subdued, even the boys.

Mrs Walker blinked back tears as she read out the register for the last time.

"Okay year six, we're going to make our way to the hall, where you're going to perform your assembly. Then we'll hand out awards, followed by lunch time. After lunch, you can go around the classrooms getting your uniforms signed, and then..."

We all knew what then.

The leaver's assembly went down *a storm*.

Our witty impressions of the teachers had the whole school in stitches, even the teachers themselves!

Mr Helix chucked when we drew attention to his constant coffee drinking.

Mrs Eve the dinner lady cackled at our impersonation of her trademark yell of *"Seconds!"* which could be heard every single lunchtime.

Mrs Barton the sports coach laughed hysterically when we demonstrated how she used to shout to lazy Annabelle: *"I don't give a flying* monkeys *if you hate sport!"*

The awards were given out for various things. Charlotte won *'The Most Horse Mad Year Six,'* although she was probably the only year six with a passion for riding. She galloped down the hall to collect her award, her face glowing its famous shade of pink.

Annabelle won the *'Glamour Queen'* award. She pouted and tossed her plaits behind her when Mrs Walker handed her the certificate.

To my surprise, my name was called under the award *'The Year Six With The Most Potential.'*

"What do I have potential for?" I asked, as I was clapped by the whole school.

"Whatever you want, Polly. You are a very sensible girl with an incredibly bright future ahead of you," Mrs Walker said. "And don't think I haven't seen you playing football with the boys in the playground. There's a definite talent there."

"Do you really think?" I breathed.

"I wouldn't say so if I didn't think it was true. Who knows, maybe you'll play for the England Ladies team one day!"

Charlotte, Annabelle and I sat by the window overlooking the playground during our last lunchtime. We talked about our fondest memories from over the past seven years.

"Do you remember when you spilt a cup of orange juice over your skirt by accident and it looked like you had wet yourself?" Annabelle said to me.

"Well, yes, but I think I remember a slightly different version - I think it was actually *you* that spilt it on me, thank you very much!" I giggled.

"Charlotte, remember that time you got sent to stand outside Mr Powell's office for chucking meatballs across the table to see if they'd bounce?"
Charlotte looked as if she might be crying, but I didn't say anything.
Annabelle sighed and gazed out of the window, lost in thought.
As Mrs Eve screeched *"Seconds!"* for the very last time, a stampede of pupils raced up to the food counter. Charlotte and I followed, and treated ourselves to a second slice of pudding. Not even Deergate's famous chocolate brownie recipe could cheer me up.

After lunch, we went round the other classrooms to have our polo shirts signed. The receptions scrawled their names across my shirt, jabbing pens into my back, but I didn't mind. I would have walked across fire if it meant prolonging time until quarter past three...

And after that, we traipsed back to the classroom for our remaining five minutes at Deergate Primary School. Seven years worth of memories filled my head as I sat on the carpet at Mrs Walker's feet surrounded by friends that had been a part of my blissful world for most of my life.
All of the girls were crying. I couldn't hold back any longer, and I began to cry too. The boys sat in silence, for once not feeling cocky.

"Year six, this is your last minute at primary school. Let's do a countdown," Mrs Walker whispered.

Every single moment of the past seven years had built up to this. No matter how hard I had tried to stop time in the past year, I had been unsuccessful, and the moment I had been too devastated to think about was finally about to happen.

The shouts got less and less enthusiastic as the numbers went down from sixty.

On 'ONE' the school bell rang, but the classroom was plunged into silence.

It was the boys who cheered first. They leapt up boisterously, barging into each other, grabbing their bags and running from classroom yelling *"HIGH SCHOOL - OH YEAH!"*

The girls shook their weeping heads in disgust.

Mrs Walker was in floods of tears herself.

"You're all lovely, *bright* girls, you'll *all* do well at Chesterlanes. Stay in touch, won't you? I am really going to *miss you.*"

One by one, we hugged her.

"Polly, you'll come back and teach me a thing or two about football, won't you?"

I nodded through my tears.

"And Charlotte, maybe I could meet Buttons again?"

"Yes, Mrs Walker," Charlotte sobbed.

"Annabelle, I hear you're going to marry a footballer? Could you introduce me to some of his friends?"

"Of course, Mrs Walker," Annabelle simpered. "Though David Beckham will be mine."

"I see," Mrs Walker chuckled. "Does Victoria know?"

"Not yet."
We all laughed, because it was easier than crying.

Annabelle's mum came to pick her up from school in their posh car - they were going straight to the airport and flying out to New York that night.
Charlotte and I held hands as if we were in reception again, and walked slowly down the school drive. We stopped systematically at the bottom of the drive and looked behind us. Deergate Primary School stood silently, alone, behind a thin canopy of oak trees, its red bricks contrasting with the dreary afternoon. The playground stood forlornly, bearing its hopscotch expectantly. The low, cheerful white fence surrounding the school was strung with flowers. It sheltered us from the outside world, kept us safe, preserved our innocence like a precious treasure. But now we stood beyond the fence. It was time to move on, grow-up.
My stomach churned with a mixture of sorrow and anticipation.
"Goodbye, Deergate. Thank you for the memories."

Cara Jasmine Bradley

Chapter Eight -
Life at Chesterlanes High School

I have now been at Chesterlanes High School for a year.
After summer, I'll be going into year eight! Time really
does fly when you're having fun.

On that first, scary day at high school, 200 eleven
year olds sat anxiously in the huge hall at the bottom of
the school, none of us sure *what* to expect.
Thrillingly, Charlotte and I found out that we were to be
in the same form. We were mixed in with a few Deergate
boys, and a range of kids from different primary schools.
I liked our form tutor Mrs Lois straight away. She was
head of the P.E department, and grinned ecstatically
when I told her I was interested in football.

A lot has changed in a year.
Charlotte and I are still best friends, though we don't
hang around with each other *all* the time.
We walk up to the bus stop together, sit next to each
other on the bus and meet up at weekends if we have
time, but we don't hang about in school.
Charlotte has befriended a group of three girls who have
their own ponies. They sit in the canteen comparing
horse photos, discussing their next ride.
She still looks very young. She wears a bit of eyeliner,
but always forgets and rubs her eyes, smudging it across
her face so that she looks like an extra from a horror film.
I still don't wear any make-up. What's the point when
it'll just get all spoiled when I play football? Besides,
I've got the rest of my life to wear make-up.

Annabelle is now best friends with a girl named
Gabriella. Gabriella does modelling for the *NEXT*

catalogues, and Annabelle says that she wants to do it too. I saw them in town together a few weeks ago, buying make-up and skirts. Annabelle has a boyfriend now. His name is Dom, and he's supposed to be the best looking boy in year seven. He's not my type. He's blonde with blue eyes, and always wears his school tie really low and has his top button undone. The teachers are always telling him off.

If I see Annabelle, I'll smile and say *'Hello,'* but I wouldn't necessarily say we're close friends anymore.

I spend most of my time at school with Francesca.

Guess what?! We both made it onto the girl's football team! It's great; we play in *proper* matches once a week, and train *twice* a week.

Dad comes to all of the matches and cheers me on at the sidelines. Mum comes whenever she can, although she stands at the opposite end of the pitch to Dad. I don't really mind, as long as they're both proud of me.

On a Wednesday, I go to Francesca's for tea, then we go training. Whenever we can, we go to the local park for a kick about. We often meet up with a few of the lads from school, including Aston, who think it's seriously cool that we play football. They don't think it's too cool when we score against them, though!

I got a Manchester City season ticket for my birthday! Dad and I go to every match, which I adore. Uncle Rob and Amber come once a month, as Aunty Elena has forbidden it any more frequently. Amber will be starting at Deergate Primary School in a few years, and I can't wait to go and watch all of her Christmas plays.

I love my life and my new, busy schedule. I have football training on Mondays and Wednesdays, and a match every Sunday. On Saturdays I go to Manchester City with my Dad, and I still go to Mum's every Friday. We have a Chinese takeaway and watch a film, or go into town and have a *McDonald's*, then I sleep over. Dad picks me up at half past 12 on Saturday afternoon to go to the match.

Mum and Dad are actually quite good friends now. They have a chat in the doorway while I get my things together. I wish they would get back together and we could go back to being the three of us, but then I remember that I'm so lucky to have such great parents that support me and love me no matter what.

Sometimes I still really miss primary school. It was particularly difficult during the first few weeks of high school. Quite often, I'd wake up thinking I was still at Deergate, and my eyes would search for the reassuring blue school jumper on the radiator. The harsh navy blue of my sharp blazer would stare back at me.

It was so strange getting off the bus after school and walking past Deergate. It seemed a thousand miles away, almost a lifetime ago since I'd been a pupil there.

One night during my first month at high school, I was in my room doing my homework, listening to the radio. The song that had been number one when I left Deergate came on. I burst into tears. I ran downstairs to Dad, who pulled me into a comforting hug. Together, we looked through all my old school photos and my Deergate memory book. I was even allowed to stay up until 10 O'clock! Dad said it was okay to cry, and that it's natural to be upset about change. He also said that

things would get better and eventually, I would stop
missing primary school so much.
At the time, I didn't believe him. I didn't see how I
would ever stop missing something so special to me...
  I still miss primary school, but not as much. What
helped me to move on was attending the Christmas fair.
Charlotte and I made that familiar route up to Deergate
one blustery Saturday morning in December. Mrs Eve
the dinner lady greeted us at the doorway with a plate of
hot mince pies. I breathed in the consoling smell of
primary school. It smelt of washing power and cooking.
Everything looked the same. Nothing had changed, but it
seemed totally alien to me. The coat pegs seemed so low
down, the brightly coloured chairs so tiny. Drawers lined
the year 6 classrooms, labelled with the names of each
pupil. I'd forgotten all about drawers. We have lockers at
high school, with our very own key!
I also couldn't imagine staying in the same room all day
long. At Chesterlanes, we moved rooms after every hour.
It was then that I realised how much *I'd* changed.
Mrs Walker was working on the lucky dip stall. She
smiled warmly when she saw us.
  "How lovely to see you again!" She exclaimed.
"No Annabelle?"
I shook my head. We had asked Annabelle to join us, but
she'd taken Gabriella up on her offer of a sleepover and
pampering session instead.
  "No Annabelle," Charlotte confirmed. "Mrs
Walker, do I look older? I've started to wear a *bit* of
make-up, and my Grandma says I'm growing up too fast,
but I'm still really small. Do you think I maybe look a *bit*
older? Do I?"

Mrs Walker laughed. "You do look a *little* older Charlotte. Have you still got Buttons?"

"Oh yes!" Charlotte beamed. That was it - once Charlotte got talking about her treasured pony, you couldn't stop her.

Mrs Walker listened obligingly, before turning to me.

"And what about you, Polly? I hope you're still into your football?"

"I'm on the school team! We won 3-0 last week, and I scored *two* goals!"

"That's brilliant! I'm so glad you've kept it up. So many people change once they go to high school. It's nice to see that you two haven't changed too much. How are you both finding it?"

"Hmm, it's *okay*. But I get home at half past four now! I used to get home at half past three when I came here. A *whole hour* earlier! Sometimes, I get back so late that I can't even ride Buttons! It's *so* stupid! Then I have thousands and *thousands* of pages of homework to do, and oh Mrs Walker, it's just a *nightmare!*"

"Well, that's life I'm afraid, Charlotte! Wait until you get a job, then you'll most likely be working nine till five! Make the most of school while you can. Do *you* like high school, Polly?"

"I do," I said carefully. "It's very *different* to primary school, but they're both good in their own ways. I love sports, but I've also really liked doing cookery. I made flapjacks last week! It's just opened up a totally different world for me."

"That's such a mature thing to say. I know that you'll have great success in whatever you do. I'm so proud of you. Of *both* of you. It's been wonderful seeing

you again."
It was so strange that Mrs Walker was talking to me like an adult. It made me feel very grown-up and somewhat proud of myself. That's when I started to feel a bit better. I'd been lucky enough to enjoy a fantastic seven years at a brilliant primary school, and now I was set to embark upon five years at high school. I was determined to make the most of every opportunity I got.

And so here I am now - the first week of the summer holidays after an eventful first year at high school. I've had a *wicked* year and made some cool new friends, as well as keeping my old ones. There have been a lot of changes, but only ones I'm happy with.
I wish I hadn't spent all that time worrying about high school.

For anyone about to make that transition from primary school to high school, I'd just like to tell you not to worry. I know it's hard to believe someone when they tell you not to worry, but I really have been in your shoes, and I *promise* that everything will be alright.

It's a sad change, and it can take you a while to get used to, but it's a change that *has* to happen. In a few years time, you'll be feeling sad about leaving *high school*, too!
High school creates so many opportunities for you, and helps to shape the person you're going to be. You don't have to forget primary school, not ever, but you have to move on. You shouldn't look back and feel sad, you should look back and feel *happy* that you had such a lovely childhood. Some children have such bad childhoods that they don't miss it at all. Think yourself

lucky that you have something worth missing.
Primary school was just one chapter in your life. You
have many more exciting chapters to come...

Printed in Great Britain
by Amazon